WITH LOVE FOR MY SISTER-IN-LAW, TRACY MYERS —S. M.

FOR MY WIFE, SONDRA —L. J.

ACKNOWLEDGMENTS

Sandra Markle would like to thank Zoe Lucas, research associate at Nova Scotia Museum, for sharing her expertise and enthusiasm for Sable Island's wild horses. A special thank-you to Skip Jeffery for his loving support throughout the creative process.

Text copyright © 2011 by Sandra Markle
Illustrations copyright © 2011 by Layne Johnson
All rights reserved. No part of this book may be reproduced or transmitted in any form or by any means, electronic or mechanical, including photocopying, recording, or by any information storage and retrieval system, without permission in writing from the publisher.

First published in the United States of America in July 2011
by Walker Publishing Company, Inc., a division of Bloomsbury Publishing, Inc.
www.bloomsburykids.com

For information about permission to reproduce selections from this book, write to
Permissions, Walker BFYR, 175 Fifth Avenue, New York, New York 10010

Library of Congress Cataloging-in-Publication Data
Markle, Sandra.
Race the wild wind : a story of the Sable Island horses / by Sandra Markle ;
[illustrations by Layne Johnson].
p.   cm.
Summary: A few horses, set free on Sable Island, Nova Scotia, soon become wild and, led by one fine stallion, find a way
to survive. Includes historical notes and facts about wild horses. Includes bibliographical references (p.   ).
ISBN 978-0-8027-9766-7 (hardcover) • ISBN 978-0-8027-9767-4 (reinforced)
1. Wild horses—Juvenile fiction. [1. Wild horses—Fiction. 2. Horses—Fiction. 3. Sable Island (N.S.)—Fiction.
4. Nova Scotia—Fiction.] I. Title.
PZ10.3.M3227Rac 2011   [E]—dc22   2010036013

Paintings created with oil on canvas
Typeset in Kepler Std Regular
Book design by Danielle Delaney

Printed in China by Toppan Leefung Printing, Ltd., Dongguan, Guangdong
2 4 6 8 10 9 7 5 3 1 (hardcover)
2 4 6 8 10 9 7 5 3 1 (reinforced)

All papers used by Bloomsbury Publishing, Inc., are natural, recyclable products
made from wood grown in well-managed forests. The manufacturing processes
conform to the environmental regulations of the country of origin.

RACE THE WILD WIND

A Story of the Sable Island Horses

SANDRA MARKLE

paintings by
LAYNE JOHNSON

Walker & Company ✦ New York

WAVES RISE UP, FALL BACK, AND RISE AGAIN,
reaching for the young stallion being lowered
from the schooner in a canvas sling.
Suddenly, whinnying and eyes white with fright,
he's free in the cold, wet sea.

Holding his head up and kicking hard,
the young stallion swims through the froth-crested waves.
He heads for a sunbright, golden arc of land—Sable Island.
Behind him, the schooner sails away.
Alongside him, other horses struggle through the surf.
Most are sturdy working breeds that plod ashore.
But the young stallion bursts onto the beach
and gallops as though in a race he was bred to win.

He snorts and rears when basking gray seals
spring to life in front of him.
Barking and wriggling, the seals stampede into the surf.
The other horses thread their way through an opening in the dunes.
The stallion trots back to them and tags along.

The horses follow their noses to autumn-gold grass
so thick and deep they have only to stand to graze their fill.
The stallion chomps the sand-crusted stalks
and whickers a complaint.
It's not the oats and sweet hay he's used to.
Still, he chews because he's hungry.
He keeps on feeding as a thick, frosty sea fog rolls ashore,
turning the horses around him into ghosts.

In the days that follow, the castaways get to know each other.
Some mares lead and others follow.
Snorting, pawing, kicking stallions battle for the mares,
taking charge of family bands.

The young stallion usually roams with other bachelors,
grazing beside them and play-fighting for practice.
But, sometimes, he runs just because he can.
Then, hooves pounding, mane flying, he races with the wind,
for no other horse can match him.

Winter arrives with sleet and snow.
To eat, the horses search for windswept patches
or paw ice-crusted snow off grasses.
To drink, they stamp to punch open ice-covered water holes.
Doing this, the young stallion throws a shoe.
He's already lost the rest, so now he runs unshod—
the way wild horses do.

Winter brings the island's fiercest weather.
Storms claw at beaches and dunes.
Family bands find a little shelter standing close together.
But it's too much for some.
When one old stallion dies, his mares are left alone.
The young stallion is the first to find them,
and he claims them for his own.

With the spring comes warmth and new life.
Grasses sprout and pond plants bloom.
Flocks of black ducks, terns, and sparrows
arrive to nest and raise their chicks.

Pregnant mares give birth to foals.
With the birth of one filly (female) and one colt (male),
the stallion's band grows bigger.

Though the island has no predators,
the young stallion keeps a constant watch for danger.
When the colt runs in play and disappears in blinding fog,
the young stallion streaks after him.
The family band waits—heads raised, ears perked—
until the young stallion returns the colt to his mother.

One late summer's eve as shadows lengthen,
a bachelor arrives, prancing and snorting, to announce his challenge.
The young stallion arches his neck and stamps his feet.
Then the rivals charge and, upon meeting,
rear and strike with teeth and hooves.
Grunting, whinnying, whirling, kicking—the stallions battle.

As quickly as it starts, it's over.
The bachelor leaves.
The stallion has proven himself a leader
and keeps his family band.

Summer turns into fall and winter comes again,
bringing the fiercest storm the horses have yet to face.
Black clouds swell bigger by the second.
Lightning flashes. Thunder booms.
Stinging rain pelts down. Waves charge ashore.
The wind ROARS!

There are no farmers to come to their rescue,
no barns for shelter.
The horses whinny in panic and run first in one direction,
then another.
The stallion bred to run now races after them.
He nips at flanks and rears until the frantic horses
are herded together and moving before him.

The horses thunder down the beach,
across wind-flattened grasses and between two mountainous dunes.
Then the stallion turns the herd, driving them up the sloping dune face
until they are just below the top.
Suddenly, monster waves curl froth and spray above them.
More water swirls below as the storm surrounds them.

Whinnying, trembling, feet stamping, heads tossing,
the horses huddle together just below the dune's crest.
There, they stay safe until the wind fades, the sea calms,
and the sun peeks through the clouds.

Only time can write the whole story of Sable Island's horses,
but one thing is for certain.
They lived to have a future that day because of the stallion
who raced against one of the island's fiercest storms
and won.

Author's Note

Race the Wild Wind was inspired by very special wild horses on Sable Island. Their history intrigued me. Some accounts suggest the first horses on the island were survivors of shipwrecks. More commonly, it's believed the horses were left behind when, in the mid-1700s, a group of people known as the Acadians were forced to leave Nova Scotia. That story tells how a wealthy Boston merchant named Thomas Hancock shipped about sixty horses, acquired from the Acadians, to Sable Island. Perhaps his goal was to let the herd graze, then collect and sell the horses. However, the merchant died and no one returned for them.

I like to think that among the hardworking farm animals, carriage horses, and riding mounts abandoned on the island, there might have been one racehorse. I can imagine what it must have been like for all of these domestic horses, especially the pampered stallion, to have to adapt to being wild. The horses had to find food and freshwater, establish social groups, and survive the fierce storms that occur on Sable Island and in this region of the Atlantic. But the horses left there did survive. In fact, they thrived. Today, the herd numbers around three hundred. And, unlike herds of untamed horses in other parts of the world, the Sable Island horses are left completely alone to roam wild and free.

Horses Are Amazing!

- Horses can sleep standing up. Unlike human leg joints that collapse when muscles relax, horses' leg joints lock in place. So their legs work together like a sling, supporting their body weight while they sleep. Most wild horses have historically been prey animals and sleeping on their feet is a natural defensive action. A standing horse can run away faster than one lying on the ground.

- A horse's hoof is a toenail, and it continues to grow throughout the horse's lifetime. Wild horses' hooves wear down naturally from walking and running across rough, hard surfaces. Domestic horses' hooves are covered by shoes, so the hooves have to be trimmed every four to eight weeks.

- Horses have small stomachs that let the food pass through in as little as fifteen minutes. Their food contains more fiber than nutrients. Small stomachs allow them to process the large amount of food they eat each day to get the energy they need.

- A horse chews by moving its lower teeth back and forth against its upper teeth. A horse's teeth erupt, or continue to move down below the gum line, as chewing wears down the grinding surface. A horse's teeth will last well into old age. Researchers are continuing to study how eating sand-crusted grass affects the teeth of Sable Island's horses.

- A foal (baby horse) develops for eleven months before it's born. Within just one to two hours after birth, it can stand and walk.

To find out more about wild horses around the world, check out these books and websites.

Books

Bastedo, Jamie. *Free as the Wind: Saving the Horses of Sable Island*. Illustrated by Susan Tooke. Calgary, Alberta, Canada: Red Deer Press, 2007.

> This fictional story shares the real-life effort to save the Sable Island horses from being auctioned and slaughtered for dog food. In the 1960s, schoolchildren across Canada wrote to the country's prime minister, pleading for the lives of these wild horses. Eventually, their effort was successful.

Jauck, Andrea, and Larry Points. *Assateague: Island of the Wild Ponies*. Mariposa, California: Sierra Press, 2007.

> Investigate wild horses living on Assateague Island. Compare their lives to those of the wild horses living on Sable Island.

Swanson, Diane. *Welcome to the World of Wild Horses* (Welcome to the World series). Toronto, Canada: Walrus Books, 2002.

> Dynamite full-color photos and facts combine to provide an introduction to the lives of wild horses.

Websites

What Happened to the Animals?

http://museum.gov.ns.ca/mnh/nature/sable/index.htm

> Discover the history of the animals living on Sable Island, including its wild horses.

Sable Island

http://museum.gov.ns.ca/mnh/nature/sableisland/english_en/nature_na/sand_sa/looking_sa.htm

> Explore Sable Island, learn its history, and see what life is like for the wild horses living there.

Sable Island Horses

http://www.greenhorsesociety.com/horses/horses.htm

> Jump to the small photos and click on the first one. This will launch you into a wonderful album, sharing insights on the lives of Sable Island's wild horses. Repeat for each of the site's other horse categories: Behavior, Foals, New Residents, Naming Horses, and Sambro. Definitely don't miss Sambro—it shares a foal's birth!

Nova Scotia

°Halifax

Sable Island